Contents

Plague!

by Nick Arnold

Series Editors: Steve Barlow and Steve Skidmore

Heinemann Educational Publishers
Halley Court, Jordan Hill, Oxford OX2 8EJ
Part of Harcourt Education

Heinemann is the registered trademark of
Harcourt Education Limited

First published 2003

07 06 05 04 03
10 9 8 7 6 5 4 3 2 1

British Library Cataloguing in Publication Data is available
from the British Library on request.

ISBN 0 435 21503 5

Illustrations by Keith Page
Cover photo by © Science Photo Library/Dr Linda Stamard UCT
Cover design by Shireen Nathoo Design
Designed and typeset by Artistix, Thame, Oxon
Printed and bound in Great Britain by Biddles Ltd

Original illustrations © Harcourt Education Limited, 2002

Tel: 01865 888058 www.heinemann.co.uk

Introduction

When a killer disease gets out of control, it's called a plague. Here's what a plague did to London in the year 1665.

London 1665

The street was empty and the houses were locked. On each door a red cross was painted. The cross meant that people in the house had the disease. After dark a cart rumbled down the street. The driver rang a bell. 'Bring out your dead!' he yelled. The doors opened and dead bodies were thrown onto the cart. The bodies were taken away and dumped in open pits.

In 1665, the plague killed 75,000 people. The cause was a killer disease known as Bubonic (*beuw-bon-nic*) Plague or Black Death.

A world of suffering ...

This book tells the stories of the world's worst plagues. It also tells how doctors battled against the killer diseases. Hundreds of years ago, no one knew what caused disease. Doctors risked their lives to find out what caused a plague and how to fight it. Sometimes they found vital clues. But often their cures were worse than the disease.

Now read on ... and be glad you're healthy!

The Black Death

As the ship reached the shore, the people watching gasped in horror. The deck was covered in bodies. Some bodies twitched and moaned. Others lay still. The bodies were covered in black spots and bloody sores. The Black Death was about to hit Europe!

Effects of the Black Death

The victim felt unwell

The victim had a fever

Pus-filled swellings formed in the armpits and groin. The swellings could be the size of apples

Black spots covered the body

The victim coughed blood and died

The horror begins

The ship carried merchants escaping a war in the Black Sea area. But many of them had Bubonic Plague. In three years the disease spread all over Europe. It was called the 'Black Death' from the black spots on the victims' bodies. Dirt, disease and death were part of everyday life. But this disease was worse. Far, far worse …

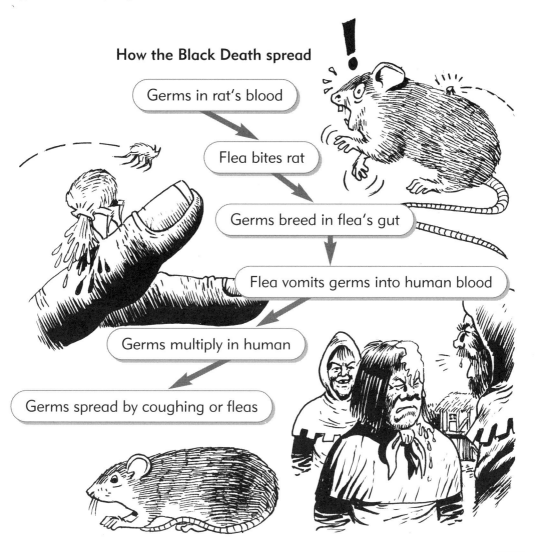

How the Black Death spread

Germs in rat's blood

Flea bites rat

Germs breed in flea's gut

Flea vomits germs into human blood

Germs multiply in human

Germs spread by coughing or fleas

Death in one day

In some places a third or half of the people died. No one felt safe. Kings locked themselves in their castles and many people left their homes. Some people fell sick and died in just one day. Fields lay empty and grass grew in city streets. Wars stopped because too many soldiers were sick or dead. In Europe the Black Death killed about 25 million people.

Was it God's anger?

Many people thought God caused the Black Death because He was angry. Thousands of people marched about the countryside. When they came to a town, they whipped themselves to show God how sorry they were. They thought God would call off the Black Death. But all they did was spread the disease and give themselves sore backs.

Hopeless cures

Doctors didn't know what caused the Black Death. Top doctors in the University of Paris came up with some ideas. They said that you could get the plague by eating olives or taking baths. Others said that bathing could ward off the disease. But you had to bathe in goat's pee. If you didn't have a goat then you could take a bath in your own pee. And drink it afterwards just to make sure.

Punishing the sick

Families with the disease were shut in their homes and left to die. Sometimes the helpers who were supposed to bring them food killed them and stole their money. In Florence, Italy, gravediggers robbed bodies and finished off sick people who were still alive.

Quarantine (kwor-an-teen)

Some sensible methods were tried. In Dubrovnik *(Doo-brov-nick)*, ships were halted. They waited thirty (later forty) days to find out if anyone on board had the disease. This stopped the disease from spreading. The Italian word for 'forty' gives us the word 'quarantine'. This means keeping someone who might have a disease away from other people.

The Black Death eases

At long last the Black Death began to ease off. Most of those too weak to fight off the disease were dead. Life became more normal. But Bubonic Plague hadn't gone away. It killed millions more victims all over Europe.

Most disease germs are ...

- Bacteria – tiny life-forms that make poisons
- Viruses – smaller than bacteria. They take over body cells and force them to make copies of the virus

Learning about germs

After 500 years of on-off Bubonic Plague, scientists found out that disease was caused by germs. In 1894, Bubonic Plague was killing millions of people in China. But this time, scientists were hot on its trail ...

Hong Kong, 1894

The disease detective

Alexandre Yersin was working late. He was in his lab – a straw hut in the grounds of the Alice Memorial Hospital. It was a hot evening and the air was filled with the stink of rotting bodies. Yersin was searching for the Bubonic Plague germ, but he knew it was a long shot. Millions of bacteria live in the body. But which of them caused Bubonic Plague?

A sickening task

Yersin bribed gravediggers to let him cut the swellings from bodies. Then he injected bacteria from the swellings into rats. He knew the danger. If he found the germ, it could kill him.

Then at last a rat got sick. Was it the Bubonic Plague? Yes! Yersin peered down his microscope in horrified triumph. He saw an unknown type of bacteria. He was the first person to see the killer germs.

The battle begins

That was only the start. It took Yersin several years to make a drug. The drug had to block the poisons made by the Bubonic Plague germ. But he did it, and today the disease can be cured.

Miracle drugs

The most powerful drugs that kill bacteria are called antibiotics *(an-tee-bi-ot-tics)*. They were first found in a mould. Mould is the greenish stuff that grows on stale bread. It's a kind of fungus.

The Blue Death

It was carnival time. Fireworks blasted and lit up the evening sky. People in weird masks and bright costumes danced through the streets. Suddenly a musician fell twitching into the gutter. His face was a purple-blue colour. It looked like a mask, but it was the man's skin. Foul, runny gut fluids leaked from his trousers.

Kill the foreigners!

More and more of the dancers fell over and the party broke up. Some people screamed and ran, others tried to help. Angry people gathered at street corners. They blamed foreign spies for killing the dancers. A few foreign people were grabbed and killed. Meanwhile, the sick dancers had been taken to hospital. Many were already dead. They were victims of the Blue Death or Cholera (*kol-ler-ra*).

Deadly diarrhoea

The word Cholera comes from the Greek word for 'diarrhoea' (*dyer-rear*). But Cholera is worse than the holiday squits. Cholera is diarrhoea and vomiting that kills. It goes on non-stop until the body dries out. The body turns a blue colour as the blood thickens.

By the time the victim dies, their dried-out body is black and wrinkled. Nerve damage makes the body twitch after death.

A perfect home

Cholera had spread from India, but it found a perfect home in the cities of Europe. At this time, few homes had clean water. Drinking water often came from rivers that foamed with human filth, rotting animals and rubbish. They were an ideal home for Cholera bacteria.

Bloody failures

All over Europe, thousands died. As with the Black Death, doctors had no idea what to do. Many of them thought that the illness was caused by too much blood. Doctors got rid of the blood by covering their patients in slimy, blood-sucking leeches. But taking blood made patients weaker and killed them off quicker.

Mystery in Broad Street

Cholera was still at large in Europe. In 1854 it struck a street in inner London. The water pump in Broad Street was known for its clear, refreshing water. But not any more. Everyone who drank from the pump seemed to fall sick. A London doctor, John Snow (1813–1858), thought that drinking the water caused Cholera. He found out that a public toilet was leaking into the water supply.

How Cholera spreads

A place of despair

Broad Street was a poor area. Families lived in filthy rooms. As the Cholera took hold it became a place of despair and fear. People too sick to move emptied their diarrhoea-filled pots from their windows.

Something in the water?

John Snow took some water home and left it to see what would happen. In a few days the water was scummy and foul. Perhaps something was breeding in the water? Maybe, thought Snow, this something was Cholera. Although he couldn't prove his point, Snow begged the authorities to close the pump. At last the pump was put out of action. The epidemic stopped. But it was too late to save those who had already fallen sick.

Cholera found

John Snow died without knowing for sure what caused Cholera. At last, in 1884, scientist Robert Koch (1843–1910) found Cholera bacteria in dirty water. John Snow had been proved right.

Curing Cholera

Cholera is still around in parts of the world where there's no clean water. But today the disease can be cured. Doctors now know that the best treatment is to drink clean water. Clean water, with added sugars and salts, makes up for the lost body fluids.

The Yellow Death – Yellow Fever

Cuba, 1900

Four American doctors met one evening to talk about their day's work. They were friends and made a good team. As usual, they chatted about their research. They were looking for the cause of a deadly disease.

The disease had haunted North and South America for hundreds of years. In the USA it killed thousands of victims – mostly in the south-east, but also in New York. It wrecked plans for a canal across Panama. People called it 'Yellow Fever'.

The canal of death

Frenchman, Ferdinand de Lesseps (1805–1894) wanted to build a canal between the Atlantic and Pacific Oceans. It looked easy on the map. But in the steaming jungles of Panama, the dream died.

Yellow Fever killed de Lesseps' men. Some died within days. They all had the signs of the disease. They had yellow skin, black vomit, and blood oozing from their noses and ears. Over 50,000 workers fell sick with the disease.

Within ten years all work on the canal stopped. With his dream in ruins, de Lesseps was a broken man. He spent his last years in fear of prison. Some people said he had stolen money from his company.

Were mosquitoes the answer?

Back in Cuba, cranky local doctor, Carlos Finlay, had been blaming Yellow Fever on mosquitoes for years. At first the four doctors didn't believe Finlay. They thought you could catch Yellow Fever from beds. They asked soldiers to sleep on beds stained with body waste. The waste had come from Yellow Fever victims.

The soldiers stayed healthy.

People who were shut away with the Yellow Fever victims stayed healthy too. So maybe – just maybe – Finlay was right! Perhaps a mosquito had to bite a person first?

The right bite

The four doctors decided that a mosquito was to blame for Yellow Fever. But which mozzie? There were hundreds of types to choose from! Patiently, they set mosquitoes to bite volunteers. But the volunteers stayed healthy. Then one of the doctors, James Carroll, was bitten – by accident! He fell sick with Yellow Fever.

A deadly test

The doctors had kept the mosquito. They let it bite a volunteer – a soldier named William Dean. He was very brave, because he was risking a terrible death. Sure enough, within days, Dean had Yellow Fever too.

Success and disaster

Carroll and Dean lived. Their illnesses proved that this type of mosquito spread Yellow Fever. But success was followed by tragedy. Another mosquito bit one of the doctors. Within a few days Yellow Fever had killed him.

How Yellow Fever spreads

Virus lives in monkeys

↓

Aedes (*eye-days*) mosquito bites monkey

↓

Virus is inside mosquito

↓

Mosquito bites human

↓

Human gets Yellow Fever

Man versus mosquitoes

Now the scientists had mosquitoes in their sights. It was a war without mercy. In Panama, an American Army major named Walter Gorgas took charge. He ordered the bushes where the mosquitoes hid to be burnt. All open water was covered in oil. This meant the mosquitoes couldn't lay their eggs. By 1914 almost the whole of Panama was free of Yellow Fever. At last the Canal could be finished.

The Spotted Death – Smallpox

The killer is caged in a freezing prison cell. The cell lies behind thick walls. Guards watch the prison round the clock. The killer faces execution for mass-murder.

But we're not talking about a human. It's the Smallpox virus. The cell is a container of freezing chemicals. The prison is a top-security lab.

Countless victims

No one knows how many people Smallpox has killed. It's certainly hundreds of millions. No one knows where Smallpox came from. It may have been a disease of horses or cows. Perhaps it first attacked people thousands years ago when they started farming. All we know for sure is what Smallpox did to human beings ...

Signs of Smallpox

Smallpox started with aches and pains. These quickly turned to a burning fever. Sometimes the victim spat blood and died quickly. These victims were lucky. Most suffered the pain of scores of pus-filled spots. Sometimes the whole body was a mass of spots. Other germs attacked the spots. Often chunks of the face rotted and fell away. Sometimes the skull and eye-sockets could be seen. In these cases, death was certain.

If a person got Smallpox they had a one in three chance of dying. If they lived they were often scarred for life. Some victims were left blind by the disease.

How Smallpox spread

The disease was horribly easy to catch.

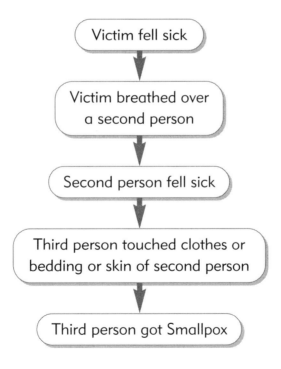

Global killer

Every year the disease killed thousands of people. No one was safe.
Smallpox killed poor people and kings and queens. Often its
victims were children. And then it went global.

In Europe and Asia there were lots of people who had had
Smallpox. Their bodies had built up defences against it. This made
it harder for Smallpox to spread. But in North and South America
and Australia, the native people had no defences. Explorers took
Smallpox all over the world. In three hundred years Smallpox
killed over one hundred million people. It was the worst plague the
world had ever known.

But humans were about to fight back.

Newgate Prison, London, 1718

You're a prisoner. You're lying on filthy straw with a chain around
your ankles. You are chained to a slimy stone wall. In a few days the
cart will arrive to take you away. You are to be hanged by the neck
until you are dead.

There's no chance of escape ...

You hear the jailer's footsteps and the jangling of his keys
without hope. The door swings open. But then the jailer makes you
an offer that could save your life ....

Here's the deal:

A lady knows of a way to protect against Smallpox. She wants you to test it. You get your arm scratched by a dirty needle that drips pus. The pus comes from a Smallpox victim. There's a chance that you'll get Smallpox and die. If you don't get Smallpox you won't be hanged. And you'll be safe from the disease for life.

Well now, what do you say?

Lady Mary's discovery

This offer was really made to six prisoners. The lady was Mary Wortley Montagu (1689–1762). Mary had a special interest in Smallpox. As a beautiful lively teenager, she had fallen ill with Smallpox. The disease had left her face with terrible scars. Mary was living in Turkey when she heard of the way to prevent Smallpox. It was dangerous. But she knew she had to try it on her own children. They lived.

Passing the test

The British government agreed to let Mary test the method on six prisoners at Newgate Prison. Once more, it worked. Soon everyone wanted to try the method. It was called inoculation (*in-nok-yew-lay-shun*). But inoculation wasn't perfect. You had a one-in-four chance of catching the disease from the Smallpox pus.

Doctor in danger

Three years later, Smallpox hit the town of Boston in America. A brave clergyman named Cotton Mather (1663–1728) urged the citizens to try inoculation. Those who tried it lived. Some people said Mather was fighting God's will. One man even tried to murder Mather.

The pus contained the Smallpox virus. The tiny dose allowed the immune system (see below) to fight the disease. If a patient caught Smallpox again, the body would be ready. The immune system would remember how to fight the disease.

The start of vaccines

Seventy-five years later, country doctor Edward Jenner (1749–1823) hit upon a better method. It was called vaccination. Jenner used a virus called Cowpox. This virus was like Smallpox, but less deadly. It also trained the body to fight Smallpox.

How vaccination (vack-sin-nay-shun) works

The human body is armed with a powerful self-defence system. Incoming germs are spotted and trapped. Then they're eaten by white blood cells. This is called the 'immune system'.

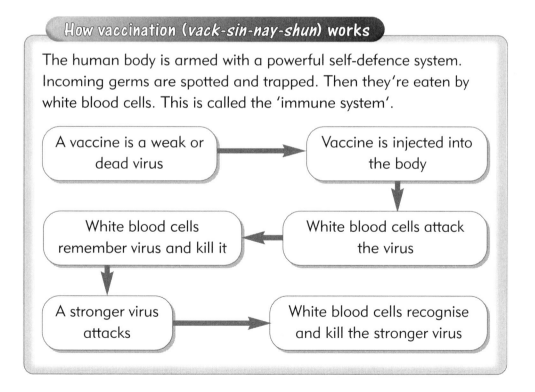

A vaccine is a weak or dead virus → Vaccine is injected into the body

White blood cells remember virus and kill it ← White blood cells attack the virus

A stronger virus attacks → White blood cells recognise and kill the stronger virus

Smallpox slashed

In country after country, vaccination slashed Smallpox rates to zero. Unlike Yellow Fever, or Black Death, the germ didn't hide in animals. If enough people were vaccinated, the germ would die out. In 1966 doctors started a world-wide push to wipe out Smallpox. The battle was on!

The mad death – Rabies (ray-beez)

Top French scientist, Louis Pasteur (1822–1895), faced a terrible choice. In 1885 he made a new vaccine for a killer disease called Rabies. Pasteur made the vaccine from the dried spinal cords of rabbits that had died of Rabies. Drying seemed to weaken the germ that caused Rabies.

How Rabies spreads

Rabies is caused by a virus

Virus multiplies in the spit of a sick animal

Animal bites another animal or human

Virus travels from the bite to the brain

Virus stops the victim drinking

Victim is scared to drink

Victims spits and dribbles and may bite

The vaccine had worked on dogs. But Pasteur wasn't sure if it would work on humans. Then a mother brought her nine-year-old son to see him. The boy, Joseph Meister, had been bitten all over by a dog. The dog had Rabies. The boy seemed doomed to die of the disease.

What should Louis Pasteur do? Give the boy the vaccine and hope it would save him? Say 'no' because the vaccine might make the boy worse? But if the boy had Rabies he would die for sure!

When Rabies got to the brain it always killed. The death was painful and horrible. Pasteur decided to try his vaccine. Joseph was given injections in his stomach. The injections really hurt but Joseph was brave. He knew the injections could save his life. Weeks passed, but Joseph stayed healthy. The vaccine had saved the boy's life!

Joseph never forgot Pasteur. When he was old enough, he worked for Pasteur. Joseph spent the rest of his life looking after the lab.

Today, a bite from an animal with Rabies means painful injections. But it doesn't mean certain death.

If you've read this far, you might think that humans have plagues beaten. You might even think that we have nothing more to fear from them.

Think that and you'd be wrong. Dreadfully, terribly wrong.

The ultimate nightmare – Ebola (ee-bo-la)

Porton Down, England, 1976

Geoff Platt worked in a top-secret lab. He worked with killer germs every day. He knew the dangers. But he also knew how to protect himself. Like other workers at Porton Down, he wore a bio-safety suit with a built-in air supply. He wore rubber gloves and kept the germs inside a sealed cabinet.

But accidents could still happen ...

Disaster strikes

On 5 November 1976, Geoff was injecting a guinea pig with germs. He wanted to find out the effects of a newly discovered virus. The needle slipped and stabbed his hand.

He'd injected himself ... with a killer disease.

The germ was Ebola. It was reckoned to be 100% deadly. Some experts called it 'the worst disease in the world'. Geoff was rushed to hospital, but he felt sure he wouldn't make it. He waited for the disease to take hold ... and kill him.

Ebola first struck remote villages in Central Africa in 1976. Doctors couldn't believe how horrible it was. It caused:
- Violent aches and pains
- Painful mouth sores
- Blood to drip from the mouth, guts, ears, nose and eyeballs
- The insides of the body to turn into a watery mush
- The skin to shrink until the face looked like a skull

The disease takes hold

All this happened to Geoff Platt. Then all his skin peeled off his body. His hair and fingernails fell out. But he was lucky to have expert nurses and the latest drugs. Amazingly, he lived!

Secrets of Ebola

Hundreds of people have died of Ebola in Africa. No-one knows where the disease came from. It might have been an ape virus that spread to humans. But Ebola is hard to catch. The only way you can get it is to touch the body wastes or blood of a victim. It can't be breathed in like a cold virus.

But the Ebola virus is just one of many new diseases that have appeared in the last few years. Scientists aren't sure why this is happening. It could be because more people are living in forests. This means there is more chance of catching diseases from wild animals.

AIDS – the silent killer

Since the 1980s the world has been hit by a terrible disease. It's called HIV – Human Immunodeficiency (*im-mew-no-deff-ish-en-sy*) Virus. Unlike other germs, HIV doesn't attack the body directly. It hides inside the body's defence force, the white blood cells. Over many years HIV wipes out the body's defences until they can't hold off other killer germs. This is called AIDS – Acquired Immune Deficiency Syndrome.

AIDS is hard to get. The HIV virus can only be picked up from blood or body fluids. That means you won't catch it by kissing or sharing a toothbrush or sitting on a toilet seat!

Searching for a cure

The HIV virus was found by French scientists in 1984. Since then, scientists have worked on many possible treatments. But none of these drugs is 100% effective.

Meanwhile, tens of millions of people, mostly in Africa, have caught the HIV virus. HIV is a killer. Over 99% of those with the virus will die unless a cure is found.

A healthy future?

Inoculation and vaccination were great victories for humans over disease. But now we face the threat of new plagues, such as HIV. In 1979, doctors celebrated as they claimed Smallpox had been wiped out. Yet some Smallpox germs remain in top-security labs in the USA and Russia.

There are real fears that terrorists could get hold of Smallpox. If they ever do, the result would be mass-murder. Since 1979, millions of people have grown up without vaccination. Their bodies have no defence against the killer disease. If Smallpox escaped, one billion people could die.

This book has shown how humans have made great steps forward in defeating disease. But humans can be their own worst enemies. In the future battle against plagues, the danger may come from within – not from the plagues we discover, but from the plagues we set free.